My Whole Self Before YOU

A Picture Prayer Book
Modeled after
the Lord's Prayer

Susan Case Bonner

Kid Niche
PUBLISHING
Traverse City, MI

Published by Kid Niche Publishing, Traverse City, MI
www.kidniche.com

Publisher's Cataloging-Publication Data
Bonner, Susan Case.

My whole self before you : a picture prayer book modeled after the Lord's prayer /
Susan Case Bonner. – Traverse City, MI : Kid Niche Pub., 2012.

p. ; cm.

ISBN13: 978-0-9852712-1-3

1. Lord's prayer. 2. Children—Prayers and devotions. 3. Children—Religious life. I. Title.

BV23 2.B66 2012

226.9606—dc23   2012943737

Project coordination by Jenkins Group, Inc.
www.BookPublishing.com

Cover and interior design: Eric Tufford
Manuscript Editor: Rebecca Chown

Special thanks to Baseline United Methodist Church for permission to use the stained glass images of the Good Shepherd and a Mother's Love. They are sections of stained glass windows that are part of this old stone church building between Battle Creek and Bellevue, Michigan. A grateful nod to David Vandlen, the artist who created these lovely windows.
The stained glass windows on pages 6–7 are part of Stanford Memorial Church
at Stanford University in California and St. James Parish Church in Barbados.

Ongoing thanks to my husband, Keith, for the contributions he has made in the form of supportive encouragement, ideas that were better than mine, and the gentle love he daily showers on me.
Without his help, I would not be able to function as effectively in the world of creativity.

Printed in the United States by Worzalla Publishing, First Printing, August 2012

16 15 14 13 12 • 5 4 3 2 1

Author's Note: The version of the Lord's Prayer used in this book (minus the doxology) is based on the wording that King Henry VIII established as the standard for all English speaking people in the sixteenth century before breaking ties with the Roman Catholic Church. It is patterned after William Tyndale's translation of 1525. All other Bible quotations are taken directly from the New American Standard Bible of 1971.

Jesus said to them, "Permit the children to come to Me; do not hinder them; for the kingdom of God belongs to such as these."

Mark 10:14

To: _____

From: _____

On the occasion of: _____

_____

Date: _____

Dedication

To my daughter, Katherine,
whose pure and simple love for Jesus
inspired this prayer.

To my son, Justin,
whose tender heart and impish ways
reinforced the need for this prayer.

Dear Father
in heaven,

I come
and I bow

my whole self
before you.

Please hear me
right now.

1

I'm glad that
you love me.

I'm glad that
you care

for me and
my family

and folks
everywhere.

I'm glad you sent Jesus. I know he's your Son.

I'm learning about all the things he has done—

Like living

and dying

and living again,

so all who receive him may live up in heav'n,

I'd like to come see you, but 'til I can come,

please help me
to do things

as you want
them done.

Please help me show kindness to others, I pray.

Please keep
me from evil

and help
me obey.

Please give
me those
things, God,

you know
that I need,

15

but free me from

selfishness,
pouting,
and greed.

17

And for all the
bad things

I say and
I do,

forgive me and
teach me

to be more
like you.

Thank you,
dear Father,

and

thank you
again—

to you be
all glory
forever.

Amen.

My Whole Self Before YOU

Dear Father in heaven, I come and I bow
my whole self before you. Please hear me right now.

I'm glad that you love me. I'm glad that you care
for me and my family and folks everywhere.

I'm glad you sent Jesus. I know he's your Son.
I'm learning about all the things he has done —

Like living and dying and living again,
so all who receive him may live up in heav'n.

I'd like to come see you, but 'til I can come,
please help me to do things as you want them done.

Please help me show kindness to others, I pray.
Please keep me from evil and help me obey.

Please give me those things, God, you know that I need,
but free me from selfishness, pouting, and greed.

And for all the bad things I say and I do,
forgive me and teach me to be more like you.

Thank you, dear Father, and thank you again —
to you be all glory forever. Amen.

Side by Side Comparison to the Lord's Prayer

The Lord's Prayer (Our Father)	My Whole Self Before YOU
Our Father who art in heaven,	Dear Father in heaven,
Hallowed be thy name.	I come and I bow my whole self before you.
Thy kingdom come. Thy will be done on earth as it is in heaven.	I'd like to come see you, but 'til I can come, please help me to do things as you want them done.
Give us this day our daily bread.	Please give me those things, God, you know that I need.
And forgive us our trespasses, as we forgive those who trespass against us.	And for all the bad things I say and I do, forgive me and teach me to be more like you.
And lead us not into temptation, but deliver us from evil.	Please keep me from evil and help me obey.
(Doxology) For Thine is the kingdom, and the power, and the glory forever. Amen.*	To you be all glory forever. Amen.

* "For Thine is the kingdom, and the power, and the glory forever. Amen" is a version of a song-like phrase early Christians recited as a praise ending to the Lord's Prayer. Whether it was part of the original prayer Jesus taught his followers is questioned, because it is not found in the earliest manuscripts of the book of Matthew. This short verse of praise is called a doxology and is based on I Chronicles 29:11.

"I love the Lord, because He hears my voice and my supplications. Because he has inclined His ear to me, therefore I shall call upon Him as long as I live."

Psalm 116:1-2

A Word from the Author

I wrote *My Whole Self Before You* as a teaching prayer for my young daughter Katherine, blending Jesus' timeless concepts from the Lord's Prayer with her simple way of saying things. Although longer than a typical child's prayer, Katherine not only prayed the words with enthusiasm and meaning, she also memorized all the verses effortlessly. This prayer became the tangible framework for helping her grow in her understanding of who God is and how to talk to him.

It is with joy that I now pass this tool along to others who also desire to teach their children the skill of meaningful prayer — one of the few skills that has both tangible and eternal benefits. May this resource help launch your children into lives that are enriched by meaningful and effective conversations with God.

 With love for you and yours,

Susan Case Bonner

Susan Case Bonner graduated from Columbia International University in Columbia, South Carolina, with a bachelor's degree in Biblical Education. As a Christian school teacher, home school teacher, Christian education director, Sunday school teacher, chapel and conference speaker, and parent of two children, she has dedicated the last thirty-five years of her life to teaching the Bible simply and creatively so that children of all ages can understand and embrace its teachings.

Susan currently writes and publishes children's books in Traverse City, Michigan, with her husband Keith. She is actively involved in her home church and enjoys interior design, thrift shopping, and antiquing.

Companion Bible lessons are available for this prayer at www.kidniche.com.

Journal

Date: _____

Prayer / Answer / Insight: _____
_____
_____
_____

Date: _____

Prayer / Answer / Insight: _____
_____
_____
_____

Date: _____

Prayer / Answer / Insight: _____
_____
_____
_____

Date: _____

Prayer / Answer / Insight: _____
_____
_____

Date: _____

Prayer / Answer / Insight: _____
_____
_____
_____

Date: _____

Prayer / Answer / Insight: _____
_____
_____
_____

Date: _____

Prayer / Answer / Insight: _____
_____
_____
_____

Date: _____

Prayer / Answer / Insight: _____
_____
_____

Journal

Date: _____

Prayer / Answer / Insight: _____

_____

_____

_____

Date: _____

Prayer / Answer / Insight: _____

_____

_____

_____

Date: _____

Prayer / Answer / Insight: _____

_____

_____

_____

Date: _____

Prayer / Answer / Insight: _____

_____

_____

Date: _____

Prayer / Answer / Insight: _____

_____

_____

_____

Date: _____

Prayer / Answer / Insight: _____

_____

_____

_____

Date: _____

Prayer / Answer / Insight: _____

_____

_____

_____

Date: _____

Prayer / Answer / Insight: _____

_____

_____